LIVE IN THE LIGHT
a journal of self-enlightenment

Illustrated by
Mary Engelbreit

Andrews McMeel
Publishing

Kansas City

MARY ENGELBREIT

Live in the Light:
A Journal of Self-Enlightenment

For information write Andrews
McMeel Publishing,
4520 Main Street,
Kansas City, Missouri 64111.

www.maryengelbreit.com

ISBN: 0-7407-3977-8

Edited by Marti Petty
Design by Stephanie R. Farley

Light is the symbol of truth.

James Russell Lowell

LIVE IN THE LIGHT

I am one of those
who never knows the direction of my journey
until I have almost arrived.

Anna Louise Strong

In the right light,
at the right time,
everything is extraordinary.

Aaron Rose

You never know
what you can do
till you try.

English proverb

He whom love touches not
walks in darkness.

Plato

A friend is someone
who reaches for your hand,
but touches your heart.

Kathleen Grove

A cheerful friend
is like a sunny day
spreading brightness
all around.

John Lubcock

Give what thou hast,
then shalt thou receive.

anonymous

It's loving and giving
that makes life worth living.

anonymous

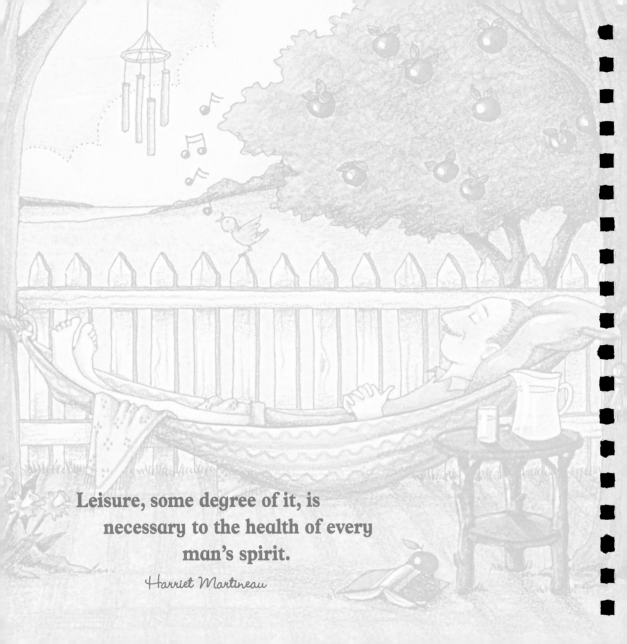

Leisure, some degree of it, is
necessary to the health of every
man's spirit.

Harriet Martineau

To be awake is to be alive.

Henry David Thoreau

Beauty seen is never lost,
God's colors all are fast.

John Greenleaf Whittier

Draw your strength from who you are.

Russel Means

Scatter seeds of kindness
everywhere you go;
scatter bits of courtesy—
watch them grow.

Amy R. Raabe

Walk towards the sunshine,
and the shadows
will fall behind you.

anonymous

It is only with the heart
that one can see rightly;
what is essential
is invisible to the eye.

Antoine de Saint Exupery

We must never be afraid to go too far,
for success lies just beyond.

Marcel Proust

**Look for
what is good
and you will find it.**

anonymous

While walking examine the walking;
 while sitting, the sitting . . .

Zen saying

Just do what you do best.

Red Auerbach

Friends are the
sunshine of life.
John Hay

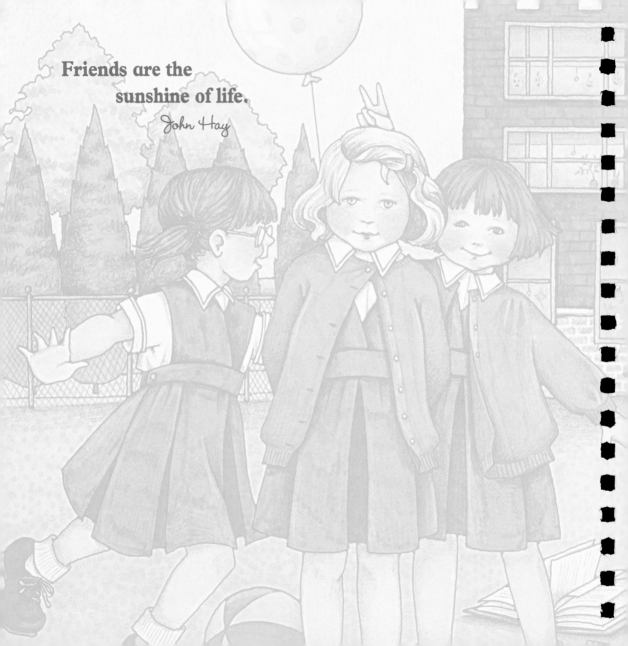

Never ask more or less of yourself
than your best.

proverb